Awake Thou Who...

John Wesley's ...

In T...

Copyright 201. ...shing

First Edition Published in 2.. ...greaves Publishing

Original sermon written by John Wesley, and is in the Public Domain. James Hargreaves has asserted his right to be identified as the author of this work in accordance with the Copyright, Designs and Patents Act 1988.
Hargreaves Publishing, England.

www.hargreavespublishing.com

www.facebook.com/hargreavespublishing

www.twitter.com/hargreavesbooks

Contents

Translator's preface

John Wesley led one of the greatest Christian revivals in the history of England, and his open air preaching saw many thousands of conversions all across Great Britain. The 'Forty-Four Sermons' which he compiled for use by Methodist Local Preachers remains a timeless classic, and a definitive collection of core Wesleyan doctrine, along with his Notes on the New Testament.

Forty-Four Sermons was first published in 1759, over 250 years ago, and since then the English language has changed and evolved to the point that his works can no longer be easily read and understood in their original dialect. Therefore to preserve Wesley's message and to allow it to come to life for a new generation, this project has been undertaken.

Many of John and Charles Wesley's views can be seen as products of the day and age in which they lived. The passion they preached with, and the relentless conviction behind their words changed Britain, some say prevented a civil uprising and revolution, and in many ways influenced the whole world. However, by today's standards, certain parts of their preaching might in places come across as uncomfortable, questionable, or even downright offensive to some readers, the modern church being as broad and diverse in theological variety as it is.

I would firstly like to state that anything I have translated and paraphrased into the modern vernacular from Wesley's writings does not necessarily represent my views, but rather the views of the original writer, in the setting of their culture and place in history. I would secondly like to state that I have not reproduced these writings with any agenda, but rather for the sake of devotional study and academic curiosity concerning their doctrines and beliefs.

The sermons are translated sentence by sentence, carefully and prayerfully. The aim has been to communicate both word-for-word and thought-for-thought, choosing clarity of communication in simple English over archaic sentence structure where necessary, and preferring the original word order when there is no difference.

Wesley used the King James Bible in his original sermons, whereas to remain consistent with the word-for-word and thought-for-thought method used in these translations, the New International Version and New Living Translation have been used instead. Gender inclusive language has also been favoured over the archaic use of the word 'he' to indicate 'everyone'. The word 'humanity' has also been favoured over the word 'mankind', as this latter word now carries with it gender implications which were not present in Wesley's time. The complete original sermon is also included. Each time scripture is directly quoted, it is italicised.

Each sermon will be translated and published in order, from 1 to 44, and when the series is completed, they will be published as one volume.

In the meantime, I hope you are blessed, encouraged and challenged by the message of John Wesley, the man who completely changed the nation in which he lived. I hope you are spurred on to a zealous faith as you read how radical he was, and look back on the incredible fruit which his approach to Christian living bore for the Kingdom of God.

In Christ,

James Hargreaves

Wake Up, Sleeper! (In Today's English)

Sermon 3 of 44

Introduction

Preached on Sunday April 4, 1742, before the University of Oxford, by the Rev. Charles Wesley, M.A. student of Christ-Church

"Awake, O sleeper, rise up from the dead, and Christ will give you light." Eph 5:14

As I discuss this passage, with God's help I will explain;

Firstly; the identity of the sleepers to whom this verse is speaking,

Secondly; the challenge to 'wake up!'

And

Thirdly; the promise of God for those who awaken; that

"Christ will give them light."[1]

---

[1]   In discoursing on these words, I shall, with the help of God, --
First. Describe the sleepers, to whom they are spoken:

Secondly. Enforce the exhortation, "Awake, thou that sleepest, and arise from the dead:" And,

Thirdly. Explain the promise made to such as do awake and arise: "Christ shall give thee light."

Who Are The Sleepers?

1:1. Firstly, we will discuss the identity of the 'sleepers.' The word 'sleep' describes the initial state of all humanity. It represents that deep soul-sleep to which Adam condemned all his descendents when he sinned in the Garden of Eden. It brings apathy, laziness and stupidity to the sleepers, making them completely oblivious of the condition into which they were born and remain (until God wakes them up).[2]

1:2. 1 Thessalonians 5:7 states that *'Night is the time when people sleep,'* and Isaiah 60:2 says; *'Darkness as black as night covers all the nations of the earth.'* The Bible shows that the world is naturally in a state of total darkness. Sinful humanity, fast asleep in this darkness can know all there is to

---

[2]   1. And first, as to the sleepers here spoken to. By sleep is signified the natural state of man; that deep sleep of the soul, into which the sin of Adam hath cast all who spring from his loins: That supineness, indolence, and stupidity, that insensibility of his real condition, wherein every man comes Into the world, and continues till the voice of God awakes him.

know about external things, but can't know anything at all about themselves. It is just as 1 Corinthians 8:2 states;

'Anyone who claims to know all the answers doesn't really know very much.'[3]

People don't realise that they were born into fallenness and that their highest priority in life is to be restored to the image of God in which they were created. They don't think they need the only thing they truly do need; the complete internal change that comes from being born again. This happens in baptism, which begins restoration, cleansing and rededication to God of the spirit, soul and body, without which no-one will see Him (Heb 12:14).[4]

---

[3]   2. Now, "they that sleep, sleep in the night." The state of nature is a state of utter darkness; a state wherein "darkness covers the earth, and gross darkness the people." The poor unawakened sinner, how much knowledge soever he may have as to other things, has no knowledge of himself: in this respect "he knoweth nothing yet as he ought to know."

[4]   he knows not that he is a fallen spirit, whose only business in the present world, is to recover from his fall, to regain that image of God wherein he was created. he sees no necessity for the one thing needful, even that inward universal change, that "birth from above," figured out by baptism, which is the beginning of that total renovation. that sanctification of spirit, soul, and body, "without which no man shall see the Lord."

1:3. Sleepers are full of every kind of sickness yet believe they are in perfect health. Locked up tight in chains of misery, they believe themselves to be free. They tell one another, 'Relax! Don't worry!" while the devil, like a strong and heavily armed man, takes possession of their souls. They sleep on, getting all the rest they want even as Hell itself rises out of the depths to meet them; even though the abyss of no return yawns wide to swallow them whole. The flames rise all around them, but they don't realise it. Their skin begins to burn and still they notice nothing.[5]

1:4. It can be seen therefore, that a 'sleeper' is a sinner who is perfectly happy in their life of sin. It is someone who has no problem at all with staying in their fallen state, and is content

---

[5]   3. Full of all diseases as he is, he fancies himself in perfect health. Fast bound in misery and iron, he dreams that he is at liberty. he says, "Peace! Peace!" while the devil, as "a strong, man armed," is in full possession of his soul. he sleeps on still and takes his rest, though hell is moved from beneath to meet him; though the pit from whence there is no return hath opened its mouth to swallow him up. A fire is kindled around him, yet he knoweth it not; yea, it burns him, yet he lays it not to heart.

to live and to die without ever becoming what they were meant to be; in the image of God. It is someone who neither knows that they are ill nor has heard of the remedy they need. It is someone who was never warned, or perhaps never paid attention to the warnings they did receive concerning the terrible wrath of God's to come. The sleepers have never realised that they are in danger of the flames of hell, nor have they ever cried out to God from the bottom of their hearts, 'What must I do to be saved?'[6]

1:5. If the sleeper doesn't act in a violent or disruptive way, that person's sleep is usually the deepest of all. They might be like the Laodiceans in Revelation 3:15, being *'neither hot nor cold,'* instead being quiet, rational, inoffensive and good-

---

[6]   4. By one who sleeps, we are, therefore, to understand (and would to God we might all understand it!) a sinner satisfied in his sins; contented to remain in his fallen state, to live and die without the image of God; one who is ignorant both of his disease, and of the only remedy for it; one who never was warned, or never regarded the warning voice of God, "to flee from the wrath to come;" one that never yet saw he was in danger of hell-fire, or cried out in the earnestness of his soul, "What must I do to be saved"

natured students of the Christian religion, but not passionate followers of it. Alternatively, at the other end of the scale they might be zealous and strict; they might be *'members of the Pharisees, the strictest sect of our religion'* (Acts 26:5), which means they try to earn righteousness and acceptance from God by their own works.[7]

1:6. A Pharisaic kind of person *'acts religious, but rejects the power that could make them godly'* (2 Tim 3:5). Indeed, they probably ridicule and reject the power of God whenever it is found, labelling it the attention-seeking behaviour of fanatics. At the same time, these pitiful self-deceived people actually **thank** God for the way they are, saying things like: *'I am not a sinner like everyone else. For I don't cheat, I don't sin, and*

---

[7]   5. If this sleeper be not outwardly vicious, his sleep is usually the deepest of all: whether he be of the Laodicean spirit, "neither cold nor hot," but a quiet, rational, inoffensive, good-natured professor of the religion of his fathers; or whether he be zealous and orthodox, and, "after the most straitest sect of our religion," live "a Pharisee;" that is, according to the scriptural account, one that justifies himself; one that labours to establish his own righteousness, as the ground of his acceptance with God.

I don't commit adultery… I fast twice a week, and I give you a tenth of my income (Lk 18:11-12). They do all the good they can so that as far as obeying the law goes they are blameless. They have every element of godliness except the power of God. They have every element of true religion, except the very essence of it. They have every element of Christianity, except Christ, who is the truth and the life.[8]

1:7. Do you realise that no matter how respected and admired such a Christian might be, they are detestable to God, and will inherit every curse that the Son of God (who is the same yesterday, today and forever) spoke against the Scribes, Pharisees and hypocrites? They too wash the outside of the

---

[8]   6. This is he, who, "having a form of godliness, denies the power thereof;" yea, and probably reviles it, wheresoever it is found, as mere extravagance and delusion. Meanwhile, the wretched self-deceiver thanks God, that he is "not as other men are; adulterers, unjust, extortioners": no, he doeth no wrong to any man. he "fasts twice in a week," uses all the means of grace, is constant at church and sacrament, yea, and "gives tithes of all that he has;" does all the good that he can "touching the righteousness of the law," he is "blameless": he wants nothing of godliness, but the power; nothing of religion, but the spirit; nothing of Christianity, but the truth and the life.

cup and leave the inside filthy (Lk 11:39). An evil sickness is still clinging to them and on the inside they are very wicked. Jesus rightly says to them, *'You are like whitewashed tombs, which look beautiful on the outside but on the inside are full of dead men's bones and everything unclean.'*[9]

However, their dead bones are no longer dusty and dry. Muscles and flesh have grown around them and they are covered with a body of skin, but there is no life in them, nor is the Holy Spirit in them. Romans 8:9 tells us *'those who do not have the Spirit of Christ living in them do not belong to him at all'* and *'You are controlled by the Spirit if you have the Spirit of God living in you.'* If you do not have the Holy Spirit in

---

[9]   7. But know ye not, that, however highly esteemed among men such a Christian as this may be, he is an abomination in the sight of God, and an heir of every woe which the Son of God, yesterday, to-day, and for ever, denounces against "scribes and Pharisees, hypocrites" he hath "made clean the outside of the cup and the platter," but within is full of all filthiness. "An evil disease cleaveth still unto him, so that his inward parts are very wickedness." Our Lord fitly compares him to a "painted sepulchre," which "appears beautiful without;" but, nevertheless, is "full of dead men's bones, and of all uncleanness."

you, then you exist in a living death which continues to this very moment.[10]

1:8. Sleepers are already dead and don't know it. They are dead to God because of their disobedience and many sins (Eph 2:1). Paul discusses this in Romans 8:6, saying; *'letting your sinful nature control your mind leads to death'*, and also in Romans 5:12 where he states, *'When Adam sinned, sin entered the world. Adam's sin brought death, so death spread to everyone'*.[11]

This isn't only a bodily death, but also an eternal spiritual death. *'You must not eat from the tree of the knowledge of*

---

[10] The bones indeed are no longer dry; the sinews and flesh are come upon them, and the skin covers them above: but there is no breath in them, no Spirit of the living God. And, "if any man have not the Spirit of Christ, he is none of his." "Ye are Christ's, if so be that the Spirit of God dwell in you": but, if not, God knoweth that ye abide in death, even until now.

[11] 8. This is another character of the sleeper here spoken to. he abides in death, though he knows it not. he is dead unto God, "dead in trespasses and sins." For, "to be carnally minded is death " Even as it is written, "By one man sin entered into the world, and death by sin; and so death passed upon all men;"

good and evil,' God said to Adam, *'for when you eat of it you will surely die.'* This was obviously not a threat of physical death, because Adam lived on (unless by physical death we mean falling from immortality as he did). If we accept that immediate physical death was not what God meant, then we may assume Adam's death was therefore spiritual. I believe that the curse meant 'your soul will die' and 'you will be dead to God,' it meant that Adam would be separated from the Father and from the essential life and happiness which He gives.[12]

1:9. That is how the vitally important connection of our souls with God was severed, so that even though we live physically, we are spiritually dead. In this state we must remain until the Second Adam, that is Jesus (1 Cor 15:45), comes as a life-

---

[12]   not only temporal death, but likewise spiritual and eternal. "In that day that thou eatest," said God to Adam, "thou shalt surely die;" not bodily (unless as he then became mortal), but spiritually: thou shalt lose the life of thy soul; thou shalt die to God: shalt be separated from him, thy essential life and happiness.

giving Spirit to us, breathing life to those who are spiritually

dead in sin, pleasures, riches or personal glory.[13]

Before any dead soul can be brought back to life however,

first they must listen to the voice of Jesus, and before they

will listen to Him, first they must realise that they are lost

souls under the death sentence. They must accept that they are

dead, even though their bodies are alive; dead to God and

everything to do with Him; as incapable of living as a

Christian as a corpse is of living as a human.[14]

1:10. Those who are spiritually dead and living in sin

certainly have not *'trained themselves to distinguish good*

---

[13]　　9. Thus first was dissolved the vital union of our soul with God; insomuch that "in the midst of" natural "life, we are" now in spiritual "death." And herein we remain till the Second Adam becomes a quickening Spirit to us; till he raises the dead, the dead in sin, in pleasure, riches or honours.

[14]　　But, before any dead soul can live, he "hears" (hearkens to) "the voice of the Son of God": he is made sensible of his lost estate, and receives the sentence of death in himself. he knows himself to be "dead while he liveth;" dead to God, and all the things of God; having no more power to perform the actions of a living Christian, than a dead body to perform the functions of a living man.

from evil' (Heb 5:14). Because they have not trained themselves, though they have eyes and ears they cannot recognise right from wrong in anything they see or hear. Because they don't know what is right, they never come to God where they might *'taste and see that He is good'* (Ps 34:8). They have no idea of what Jesus is like, of the power of His words or the historical fact of His existence as a physical person (1 John 1:1).[15]

It doesn't occur to them that Jesus is the purest source of joy-giving righteousness, nor how majestic and desirable it is to be with God (Psalm 45:7-8). The soul that is sleeping in death cannot see any of it. That heart is beyond all feeling, and cannot understand these things at all.[16]

---

[15] 10. And most certain it is, that one dead in sin has not "senses exercised to discern spiritual good and evil." "Having eyes, he sees not; he hath ears, and hears not." he doth not "taste and see that the Lord is gracious." he "hath not seen God at any time," nor "heard his voice," nor "handled the word of life."

[16] In vain is the name of Jesus "like ointment poured forth, and all his garments smell of myrrh, aloes, and cassia." The soul that sleepeth in death hath no perception of any objects of this kind. his heart is "past feeling," and understandeth none of these things.

1:11. Human beings in their natural condition have no spiritual senses at all, and therefore cannot grow in spiritual knowledge or receive the things of the Holy Spirit. They are so far from being able to receive such things, that if they ever hear real spiritually-discerned truth, it sounds ridiculous and foolish to them.

They are not satisfied merely with being ignorant of spiritual things however, and go even further, denying their very existence. The ability to discern spiritual things, such as their own condition, sounds like the most ridiculous thing imaginable to them.[17]

"How can it be possible," they ask, "for anyone to know whether or not they are alive to God?"

---

[17]   11. And hence, having no spiritual senses, no inlets of spiritual knowledge, the natural man receiveth not the things of the Spirit of God; nay, he is so far from receiving them, that whatsoever is spiritually discerned is mere foolishness unto him. he is not content with being utterly ignorant of spiritual things, but he denies the very existence of them. And spiritual sensation itself is to him the foolishness of folly.

"In exactly the same way you can tell whether or not your body is alive," I answer.

Faith gives life to the soul, and if you have a living soul within you, you need no external evidence to prove it to yourself, only that divine inner confirmation from God which is stronger and more meaningful than ten thousand human opinions.[18]

1:12. If you don't sense God's confirmation in your spirit that you are His child, may He powerfully prove to you, poor sleeping sinner, that you are therefore a child of the devil! If only these prophetic words would bring the sound of rattling and shaking as the dead bones join together again! (Ez 37:7) *'Come, O breath, from the four winds! Breathe into these dead bodies so they may live again'* (Ez 37:8) If you don't

---

[18] "How," saith he, "can these things be How can any man know that he is alive to God" Even as you know that your body is now alive. Faith is the life of the soul; and if ye have this life abiding in you, ye want no marks to evidence it to yourself, but elegchos pneumatos, that divine consciousness, that witness of God, which is more and greater than ten thousand human witnesses.

believe in Jesus, don't be calloused and hard-hearted; don't resist the Holy Spirit who approaches in this very moment to show you your sin.[19]

---

[19]   12. If he doth not now bear witness with thy spirit, that thou art a child of God, O that he might convince thee, thou poor unawakened sinner, by his demonstration and power, that thou art a child of the devil! O that, as I prophesy, there might now be "a noise and a shaking;" and may "the bones come together, bone to his bone!" Then "come from the four winds, O Breath! and breathe on these slain, that they may live!" And do not ye harden your hearts, and resist the Holy Ghost, who even now is come to convince you of sin, "because you believe not on the name of the only begotten Son of God."

Will You Wake Up?

2:1. Now we come to the challenge itself; *'Wake up, sleeper, and rise from the dead!'*

God is calling to you right now: His voice is calling your name. He is asking you to recognise exactly what you are: a fallen soul. That is what you are and all you should care about in this life. What do you plan to do about it, sleeper?[20] Wake up! Call out to God! If you do, He will remember you and bring you out from spiritual death. A terrible storm is rising up all around you. You are sinking down into deep damnation; into the abyss of the judged. The only way to escape God's judgement is to throw yourself upon it; judge **yourself** guilty as a sinner so you will not be judged as one by the Lord![21]

---

[20]   II. 1. Wherefore, "awake, thou that sleepest, and arise from the dead." God calleth thee now by my mouth; and bids thee know thyself, thou fallen spirit, thy true state and only concern below. "What meanest thou, O sleeper

2:2. Wake up! Wake up! Get out of your beds, in case all you ever receive from God is His wrath! Stir yourself up to find God who will make you righteous, who is mighty to save! Shake the dust off yourself! If you can't shake it off by your own willpower, let the prospect of God's judgement cause you to shake with such fear that the dust flies off! Wake up and cry out with the trembling jailer; '*What must I do to be saved?*' (Acts 16:30) Don't give up until the Holy Spirit has given you supernatural faith in Christ.[22]

2:3. I am speaking to all of you, but especially to any who think that this challenge doesn't apply to them. I have a

---

[21]   Arise! Call upon thy God, if so be thy God will think upon thee, that thou perish not." A mighty tempest is stirred up round about thee, and thou art sinking into the depths of perdition, the gulf of God's judgements. If thou wouldest escape them, cast thyself into them. "Judge thyself, and thou shalt not be judged of the Lord."

[22]   2. Awake, awake! Stand up this moment, lest thou "drink at the Lord's hand the cup of his fury." Stir up thyself to lay hold on the Lord, the Lord thy Righteousness, mighty to save! "Shake thyself from the dust." At least, let the earthquake of God's threatenings shake thee. Awake, and cry out with the trembling jailer, "What must I do to be saved" And never rest till thou believest on the Lord Jesus, with a faith which is his gift, by the operation of his Spirit.

message from God for you. In His name I warn you to *'flee God's coming wrath'* (Lk 3:7). You unholy soul, you are like Peter (in Acts 12:4), who lay condemned, bound with chains in a dark dungeon and guarded by soldiers. The night is almost over and the morning is coming when you will be brought out and executed, but despite your terrible predicament you're fast asleep! You are slumbering in the arms of the devil, teetering on the edge of the bottomless pit and about to fall into the jaws of everlasting damnation![23]

2:4. Oh, may the Angel of the Lord come to you, bringing light into your prison just as he did for Peter. May you feel the touch of the hand of Almighty God, rousing you from your sleep and saying: *'Quick, get up! Put on your clothes and*

---

[23]   3. If I speak to any one of you, more than to another, it is to thee, who thinkest thyself unconcerned in this exhortation. "I have a message from God unto thee." In his name, I warn thee "to flee from the wrath to come." Thou unholy soul, see thy picture in condemned Peter, lying in the dark dungeon, between the soldiers, bound with two chains, the keepers before the door keeping the prison. The night is far spent, the morning is at hand, when thou art to be brought forth to execution. And in these dreadful circumstances, thou art fast asleep; thou art fast asleep in the devil's arms, on the brink of the pit, in the jaws of everlasting destruction!

sandals, wrap your cloak around you and follow me' (Acts

12:7-8).[24]

2:5. You, whose spirits will live forever; wake up out of your

fantasies of superficial, selfish happiness! God created you for

Himself! You will find no peace until you come to Him and

spend your life as a true Christian.[25]

Come home, wanderers! Run back to God your fortress,

because this world is not your real home. Don't be concerned

with building a physical legacy for yourself, and don't occupy

your time pursuing praise from other people, because you are

a foreigner here; a visitor on the earth. You will only be a

creature of this planet for a very short while, and after that

time the state you enter will be permanent.[26]

---

[24]   4. O may the Angel of the Lord come upon thee, and the light
shine into thy prison! And mayest thou feel the stroke of an Almighty
Hand, raising thee, with, "Arise up quickly, gird thyself, and bind on thy
sandals, cast thy garment about thee, and follow Me."
[25]   5. Awake, thou everlasting spirit, out of thy dream of worldly
happiness! Did not God create thee for himself Then thou canst not rest till
thou restest in him.
[26]   Return, thou wanderer! Fly back to thy ark, This is not thy home.
Think not of building tabernacles here. Thou art but a stranger, a sojourner

Quickly now! Your eternal destination is just around the corner and depends on the choice you make this very moment. Do you want an eternity of happiness, or an eternity of misery?[27]

2:6. What state is your heart in? What would happen if you died this very moment? Are you ready to be judged by God? Would He whose eyes are too pure to look upon evil (Hab 1:13) be able to look upon you? Are you *'qualified to share in the inheritance of the saints in the kingdom of light'*? (Col 1:12) Have you *'fought the good fight and kept the faith'*? (2 Tim 4:7) Have you claimed the only thing you truly need? Have you returned to being in the image of God, being as righteous and truly holy as Him? (Eph 4:22-24) Have you taken off your old self and put on the new? Are you clothed with Christ?[28]

---

upon earth; a creature of a day, but just launching out into an unchangeable state.

[27]   Make haste. Eternity is at hand. Eternity depends on this moment. An eternity of happiness, or an eternity of misery!

2:7. Do you have oil in your lamp? Do you have grace in your heart? Do you *'love the Lord your God with all your heart, mind, soul and strength?'* (Mk 12:30) Do you have the same attitude as Christ Jesus? (Php 2:5) Are you a true Christian - a new creation? Has the old life gone, and a new one begun? (2 Cor 5:17)[29]

2:8. Do you *'share his divine nature'*? (2 Pet 1:4) The scriptures say: *'Surely you know that Jesus Christ is among you; if not, you have failed the test of genuine faith.'* (2 Cor 13:5) Do you know that God lives in you, and you live in God through the Holy Spirit? *'Your body is the temple of the Holy*

[28]   6. In what state is thy soul Was God, while I am yet speaking, to require it of thee, art thou ready to meet death and judgement Canst thou stand in his sight, who is of "purer eyes than to behold iniquity" Art thou "meet to be partaker of the inheritance of the saints in light" Hast thou "fought a good fight, and kept the faith" Hast thou secured the one thing needful Hast thou recovered the image of God, even righteousness and true holiness Hast thou put off the old man, and put on the new Art thou clothed upon with Christ

[29]   7. Hast thou oil in thy lamp grace in thy heart Dost thou "love the Lord thy God with all thy heart, and with all thy mind and with all thy soul, and with all thy strength" Is that mind in thee, which was also in Christ Jesus Art thou a Christian indeed, that is, a new creature Are old things passed away, and all things become new

Spirit, who lives in you and was given to you by God.' (1 Cor 16:19)[30]

Do you have that sense in your heart, the clear truth of your inheritance? Have you received the Holy Spirit? (Jn 20:22) Or does the very question make you angry? Do you even believe that there is a Holy Spirit?[31]

2:9. If this question offends you, rest assured that you that you are not a Christian and have no desire to be one. Even your prayers are a sinful offering, because you have openly mocked God by praying for His Spirit's blessing while doubting it exists.[32]

---

[30]   8. Art thou a "partaker of the divine nature" Knowest thou not, that "Christ is in thee, except thou be reprobate" Knowest thou, that God "dwelleth in thee, and thou in God, by his Spirit, which he hath given thee" Knowest thou not that "thy body is a temple of the Holy Ghost, which thou hast of God"

[31]   Hast thou the witness in thyself the earnest of thine inheritance Hast thou "received the Holy Ghost" Or dost thou start at the question, not knowing "whether there be any Holy Ghost"

[32]   9. If it offends thee, be thou assured, that thou neither art a Christian, nor desirest to be one. Nay, thy very prayer is turned into sin; and thou hast solemnly mocked God this very day, by praying for the

2:10. Yet on the authority of the Bible and the Anglican Church, I have to repeat the question, *'Have you received the Holy Spirit?'* (Acts 19:2) If you haven't, then you are not yet a Christian. I can say this with confidence because the Bible says a Christian is anointed with the Holy Spirit (1 Jn 2:20) and with power (Acts 1:8). If you have not, then you are not yet a participant in pure, holy faith.[33]

Do you know what the Christian faith is? It is sharing in the divine nature; having the life of God in your soul and Christ in your heart; it is *'Christ in you, the hope of glory.'* (Col 1:27) It is happiness and holiness. It is heaven beginning to break out upon the earth. It is the Kingdom of God which is **inside** you, not made of bricks and mortar but of

---

inspiration of his Holy Spirit, when thou didst not believe there was any such thing to be received.

[33] 10. Yet, on the authority of God's Word, and our own Church, I must repeat the question, "Hast thou received the Holy Ghost" If thou hast not, thou art not yet a Christian. For a Christian is a man that is "anointed with the Holy Ghost and with power." Thou art not yet made a partaker of pure religion and undefiled.

righteousness, peace, and joy from the Holy Spirit. It is an everlasting kingdom in your soul; the peace of God that transcends all understanding (Php 4:7) and unspeakable, glorious joy.[34]

2:11. Do you know that *'when we place our faith in Christ Jesus, there is no benefit in being circumcised or being uncircumcised?'* External rituals are not important. For a Christian, who is a new creation, *'what is important is faith expressing itself in love.'* (Gal 5:6) Do you recognise how essential is that inward change, that spiritual rebirth, that resurrection from the dead, that life of holiness? And are you totally convinced that without that inward change you will not see God? Are you striving for it?[35]

---

[34]   Dost thou know what religion is --that it is a participation of the divine nature; the life of God in the soul of man; Christ formed in the heart; "Christ in thee, the hope of glory;" happiness and holiness; heaven begun upon earth; "a kingdom of God within thee; not meat and drink," no outward thing; "but righteousness, and peace, and joy in the Holy Ghost;" an everlasting kingdom brought into thy soul; a "peace of God that passeth all understanding;" a "joy unspeakable, and full of glory"

[35]   11. Knowest thou, that "in Jesus Christ, neither circumcision availeth anything, nor uncircumcision; but faith that worketh by love;" but

Are you *'working hard to prove that you really are among those God has called and chosen?'* (2 Pet 1:10) Are you *'working hard to show the results of your salvation, obeying God with deep reverence and fear?'* (Php 2:12) Are you *'working hard to enter the narrow door to God's Kingdom?'* (Lk 13:24) Do you even care about your own soul? Can you truly tell God, who sees all your thoughts and desires, 'You, Oh God are all I want! All-knowing One, you know that I want to love you!'[36]

2:12. You hope that you can be saved, but why do you have this hope? What makes you think you might qualify for salvation? Is it because you've never hurt anyone? Is it because you have done many good deeds? Or is it because

---

a new creation Seest thou the necessity of that inward change, that spiritual birth, that life from the dead, that holiness And art thou thoroughly convinced, that without it no man shall see the Lord Art thou labouring after it

[36] "giving all diligence to make thy calling and election sure," "working out thy salvation with fear and trembling," "agonizing to enter in at the strait gate" Art thou in earnest about thy soul And canst thou tell the Searcher of hearts, "Thou, O God, art the thing that I long for! Lord, Thou knowest all things; Thou knowest that I would love Thee!"

you are not like everyone else, being wise or educated, honest or moral, popular or of good reputation? None of these things are enough! As far as God is concerned they are less than worthless and will never bring you to Him.[37]

Do you know Jesus Christ, who God sent? Do you know that *'God saved you by his grace when you believed. And you can't take credit for this; it is a gift from God. Salvation is not a reward for the good things we have done, so none of us can boast about it'*? (Eph 2:8-9) Have you accepted the truthful saying *'Jesus Christ came into the world to save sinners,'* (1 Tim 1:15) and do you know that He is the only way you can be saved?[38]

---

[37] 12. Thou hopest to be saved; but what reason hast thou to give of the hope that is in thee Is it because thou hast done no harm or, because thou hast done much good or, because thou art not like other men; but wise, or learned, or honest, and morally good; esteemed of men, and of a fair reputation Alas! all this will never bring thee to God. It is in his account lighter than vanity.

[38] Dost thou know Jesus Christ, whom he hath sent Hath he taught thee, that "by grace we are saved through faith; and that not of ourselves: it is the gift of God: not of works, lest any man should boast" Hast thou received the faithful saying as the whole foundation of thy hope, "that Jesus Christ came into the world to save sinners"

Have you learned what Jesus meant when he said; *'I came not to call the righteous, but sinners to repentance?'* (Lk 5:32) and *'I was sent only to help God's lost sheep?'* (Mt 15:24) Are you lost? Are you dead and damned already? Do you know what you deserve? Do you feel how inadequate you are? Are you *'poor in spirit?'* (Mt 5:3) Do you mourn and refuse to be comforted because you don't yet have God? (Mt 5:4)[39]

Prodigal child, are you coming to your senses? Are you willing to be regarded as a lunatic by those you leave behind to continue eating pig slop? Are you willing to live a godly life as a Christian? Are you mistreated because of your godliness? Do people make up all kinds of evil rumours against you because you are associated with Jesus?[40]

---

[39]   Hast thou learned what that meaneth, "I came not to call the righteous, but sinners to repentance I am not sent, but unto the lost sheep" Art thou (he that heareth, let him understand!) lost, dead, damned already Dost thou know thy deserts Dost thou feel thy wants Art thou "poor in spirit" mourning for God, and refusing to be comforted
[40]   Is the prodigal "come to himself," and well content to be

2:13. I pray that in these questions you would hear the voice that wakes the dead. I pray that you will feel God's word coming down upon you like a hammer that shatters mighty rocks into pieces! If you want to hear Him today, as Hebrews 3 commands, don't harden your hearts.[41]

Now, wake up you sleepers in spiritual death so that you won't sleep in eternal death! Acknowledge your lost condition and rise from the dead. Leave your old friends who encouraged you to live sinfully and follow Jesus instead. *'Let the dead bury their own dead'* (Mt 8:22). *'Save yourselves from this corrupt generation'* (Acts 2:40), *'come out from them and be separate, says the Lord. Touch no unclean thing,*

---

therefore thought beside himself" by those who are still feeding upon the husks which he hath left Art thou willing to live godly in Christ Jesus And dost thou therefore suffer persecution Do men say all manner of evil against thee falsely, for the Son of Man's sake

[41]   13. O that in all these questions ye may hear the voice that wakes the dead; and feel that hammer of the Word, which breaketh the rocks in pieces! "If ye will hear his voice to-day, while it is called to-day, harden not your hearts."

and I will receive you' (2 Cor 6:17), and *'Christ will give you light'* (Eph 5:14).[42]

---

[42]   Now, "awake, thou that sleepest" in spiritual death, that thou sleep not in death eternal! Feel thy lost estate, and "arise from the dead." Leave thine old companions in sin and death. Follow thou Jesus, and let the dead bury their dead. "Save thyself from this untoward generation." "Come out from among them, and be thou separate, and touch not the unclean thing, and the Lord shall receive thee." "Christ shall give thee light."

Christ Will Give You Light

3:1. Lastly, we will look at the promise I just mentioned that those who awake receive Christ's light. It is such an encouragement to see how this verse ends! Whoever you are, if you respond to His call you cannot seek Him and not find Him! Even now, if you awake and rise from the dead, He has bound Himself with a promise that He will give you light.[43] The Lord will give you two kinds of light: the light of grace and the light of glory. He will give you the light of His grace here on earth and the light of his glory in heaven when you receive your eternal crown. *'Your light will shine out from the darkness, and the darkness around you will be as bright as noon'* (Isa 58:10). God, who commanded light to shine out of

---

[43]   1. This promise, I come, lastly, to explain. And how encouraging a consideration is this, that whosoever thou art, who obeyest his call, thou canst not seek his face in vain! If thou even now "awakest, and arisest from the dead," he hath bound himself to "give thee light." "The Lord shall give thee grace and glory;"

the darkness when he created the world, will speak the same words over your heart. [44]

He will shine there and give you understanding of the glory of God, through Jesus. Over those who fear the Lord, *'the Sun of Righteousness will rise with healing in his wings'* (Mal 4:2) and on that day it will be said to you, *'Arise, shine, for your light has come, and the glory of the LORD rises upon you.'* (Isa 60:1) Christ will reveal that he is in you, and you will shine with His true Light.[45]

3:2. The Bible states that God **is** light. He Himself is the light which is given to every awakened sinner who waits for Him. They then become a temple of the living God with Christ

---

[44]   the light of his grace here, and the light of his glory when thou receivest the crown that fadeth not away. "Thy light shall break forth as the morning, and thy darkness be as the noon-day." "God, who commanded the light to shine out of darkness, shall shine in thy heart
[45]   to give the knowledge of the glory of God in the face of Jesus Christ." On them that fear the Lord shall "the Sun of Righteousness arise with healing in his wings." And in that day it shall be said unto thee, "Arise, shine; for thy light is come, and the glory of the Lord is risen upon thee." For Christ shall reveal himself in thee: and he is the true Light.

living in their hearts by faith. Being rooted and grounded in love they *'have the power to understand, as all God's people should, how wide, how long, how high, and how deep his love is... though it is too great to understand fully'* (Eph 3:18-19).[46]

3:3. You can see your calling brothers and sisters; we are called to be temples of the Holy Spirit. Through the Spirit living in us we are meant to be saints here on earth, and to share in the inheritance of the saints when we get to heaven. The promises which God has given to we who believe are so exceptional and wonderful, because all we need is faith to receive the Holy Spirit from God, who replaces the sinful spirit we were all born with. The indwelling of the Spirit is the fulfilment of all the promises of God in the Bible. If He lives within us, we can claim all the free gifts of God to humanity.[47]

---

[46] 2. God is light, and will give himself to every awakened sinner that waiteth for him; and thou shalt then be a temple of the living God, and Christ shall "dwell in thy heart by faith;" and, "being rooted and grounded in love, thou shalt be able to comprehend with all saints, what is the breadth, and length, and depth, and height of that love of Christ which passeth knowledge."

3:4. The Holy Spirit is the great gift of God which was promised many different times and in many different ways throughout the Bible. At Pentecost He was fully given to us at last, and those Old Testament promises made to the early fathers were fulfilled; *'I will put my Spirit in you so that you will follow my decrees and be careful to obey my regulations'* (Ez 36:27), and *'I will pour water on the thirsty land, and streams on the dry ground; I will pour out my Spirit on your offspring, and my blessing on your descendants'* (Is 44:3).[48]

---

[47]   3. Ye see your calling, brethren. We are called to be "an habitation of God through his Spirit;" and, through his Spirit dwelling in us, to be saints here, and partakers of the inheritance of the saints in light. So exceeding great are the promises which are given unto us, actually given unto us who believe! For by faith "we receive, not the spirit of the world, but the Spirit which is of God" --the sum of all the promises-- "that we may know the things that are freely given to us of God."

[48]   4. The Spirit of Christ is that great gift of God, which at sundry times, and in divers manners, he hath promised to man, and hath fully bestowed since the time that Christ was glorified. Those promises, before made to the fathers, he hath thus fulfilled: "I will put My spirit within you, and cause you to walk in My statutes" (Ezek. 36:27). "I will pour water upon him that is thirsty, and floods upon the dry ground; I will pour My Spirit upon thy seed, and My blessing upon thine offspring (Isa. 44:3).

3:5. You are all living witnesses of these promises coming true; forgiveness for sins and the indwelling of the Holy Spirit are now available. It is just as Christ said: *'Anything is possible if a person believes.'* (Mk 9:23) No-one who fears the Lord must walk in darkness any longer.[49]

I ask you, in the name of Jesus, do you believe that nothing is impossible for God? Do you believe that He is still strong enough to save anyone? Do you believe that he is the same yesterday, today and forever? Do you believe He has the power to forgive the sins of anyone on earth? If so, then *'be encouraged, my child! Your sins are forgiven'* (Mt 9:2). Because of Jesus, God has forgiven you.[50]

---

[49]   5. Ye may all be living witnesses of these things; of remission of sins, and the gift of the Holy Ghost. "If thou canst believe, all things are possible to him that believeth." "Who among you is there that feareth the Lord, and" yet walketh on "in darkness, and hath no light"

[50]   I ask thee, in the name of Jesus, Believest thou that his arm is not shortened at all that he is still mighty to save that he is the same yesterday, to-day, and for ever that he hath now power on earth to forgive sins "Son, be of good cheer; thy sins are forgiven." God, for Christ's sake, hath forgiven thee.

This is no human invention, but is the absolute word of God: you are made right with God freely by putting your faith in Him. You will also be made holy through your faith in Jesus, and God's gift of eternal life will well up in your heart.[51]

3:6. Family let me speak freely to you. I hope you will accept this challenge from me even though I occupy one of the lowest ranks in the Anglican Church. If both your conscience and the Holy Spirit confirm to you that I am telling the truth, then you have had a first taste of the grace of God. *'This is the way to have eternal life--to know the only true God, and Jesus Christ, the one he sent to earth.'* (Jn 17:3)[52]

---

[51] Receive this, "not as the word of man; but as it is indeed, the word of God;" and thou art justified freely through faith. Thou shalt be sanctified also through faith which is in Jesus, and shalt set to thy seal, even thine, that "God hath given unto us eternal life, and this life is in his Son."

[52] 6. Men and brethren, let me freely speak unto you, and suffer ye the word of exhortation, even from one the least esteemed in the Church. Your conscience beareth you witness in the Holy Ghost, that these things are so, if so be ye have tasted that the Lord is gracious. "This is eternal life, to know the only true God, and Jesus Christ, whom he hath sent."

This is a very simple test to establish true Christianity; if someone has received the Holy Spirit, they are a Christian, if they have not, then they are not a Christian. It is also impossible to have received the Holy Spirit but not know it, because Jesus said about that time when the Spirit comes, *'When I am raised to life again, you will know that I am in my Father, and you are in me, and I am in you'* (Jn 14:20). *'He is the Holy Spirit, who leads into all truth. The world cannot receive him, because it isn't looking for him and doesn't recognize him. But you know him, because he lives with you now and later will be in you.'* (Jn 14:17)[53]

3:7. The world cannot accept Him; instead they completely reject the promised Holy Spirit, contradicting the word of God

---

[53]   This experimental knowledge, and this alone, is true Christianity. he is a Christian who hath received the Spirit of Christ. he is not a Christian who hath not received him. Neither is it possible to have received him, and not know it. "For, at that day" (when he cometh, saith our Lord), "ye shall know that I am in My Father, and you in Me, and I in you." This is that "Spirit of Truth, whom the world cannot receive, because it seeth him not, neither knoweth him: but ye know him; for he dwelleth with you, and shall be in you" (John 14:17).

and blaspheming. Anyone who disagrees with me on this is not from God. *'Such a person has the spirit of the Antichrist, which you heard is coming into the world and indeed is already here'* (1 Jn 4:3). Anyone who denies the need for the power of the Holy Spirit, or who says that being filled with the Holy Spirit is not for all Christians is the Antichrist. These things are inseparable from the gospel, they are promised to all believers, and they indentify real Christians from false ones.[54]

3:8. Some of them protest: "We don't deny that the Holy Spirit helps us, we only deny this baptism in the Holy Spirit with power which can be felt. It is this awareness of the Holy Spirit within, this guidance and filling with the Spirit which

---

[54]   7. The world cannot receive him, but utterly reject the Promise of the Father, contradicting and blaspheming. But every spirit which confesseth not this is not of God. Yea, "this is that spirit of Antichrist, whereof ye have heard that it should come into the world; and even now it is in the world." he is Antichrist whosoever denies the inspiration of the Holy Ghost, or that the indwelling Spirit of God is the common privilege of all believers, the blessing of the gospel, the unspeakable gift, the universal promise, the criterion of a real Christian.

has no place in true Christianity." Protesting in this way doesn't change their status as false Christians however. In denying the baptism in the Holy Spirit, they are denying the whole Bible; the whole truth, promise and word of God.[55]

3:9. Our own excellent church, the Church of England, does not recognise any such Satanic division in our faith, but instead speaks freely about 'feeling the Spirit of Christ' (in Article 14). It also speaks of being 'moved by the Holy Spirit' (in the Office of Consecrating Priests), and of knowing and 'feeling that there is no other name than Jesus by which we receive life and salvation' (in the Visitation of the Sick).[56]

---

[55]   8. It nothing helps them to say, "We do not deny the assistance of God's Spirit; but only this inspiration, this receiving the Holy Ghost: and being sensible of it. It is only this feeling of the Spirit, this being moved by the Spirit, or filled with it, which we deny to have any place in sound religion." But, in only denying this, you deny the whole Scriptures; the whole truth, and promise, and testimony of God.

[56]   9. Our own excellent Church knows nothing of this devilish distinction; but speaks plainly of "feeling the Spirit of Christ" [Article 17]; of being "moved by the Holy Ghost" [Office of consecrating Priests] and knowing and "feeling there is no other name than that of Jesus," [Visitation of the Sick] whereby we can receive" life and salvation.

The Church teaches us all to pray for the 'filling of the Holy Spirit' (in the Collect before Holy Communion), and to pray that we might be 'filled with the Holy Spirit' (in the Order of Confirmation). Indeed, every Anglican Priest testifies that they received the Holy Spirit through the laying on of hands, so if you deny any of what I have taught today, you are effectively renouncing both the Church of England and the whole Bible.[57]

3:10. But the wisdom of God always seemed foolish to humanity. It should be no great surprise that today the mystery of the gospel is hidden from the 'wise and educated' just as it was in ancient times. True Christianity it is almost universally denied, mocked, and torn apart as fanaticism today, and anyone who dares live according to the gospel is

---

[57]   She teaches us all to pray for the "inspiration of the Holy Spirit" [Collect before Holy Communion]; yea, that we may be "filled with the Holy Ghost" [Order of Confirmation]. Nay, and every Presbyter of hers professes to receive the Holy Ghost by the imposition of hands. Therefore, to deny any of these, is, in effect, to renounce the Church of England, as well as the whole Christian revelation.

branded a 'religious lunatic' or an 'attention-seeking drama-queen.'[58]

This is that 'falling away' which the New Testament predicts. It is a general denial of true Christianity which has spread to all people of all classes in every country of the earth. Search the streets of the city and see if you can find anyone who loves the Lord their God with all their heart and serves Him with all their strength.[59]

We don't need to look beyond England to see sin overflowing and the land in mourning. Crimes of all kinds are committed every day in public by sinners proud of their actions, who too

---

[58]   10. But "the wisdom of God" was always "foolishness with men." No marvel, then, that the great mystery of the gospel should be now also "hid from the wise and prudent," as well as in the days of old; that it should be almost universally denied, ridiculed, and exploded, as mere frenzy; and that all who dare avow it still are branded with the names of madmen and enthusiasts!

[59]   This is "that falling away" which was to come--that general apostasy of all orders and degrees of men, which we even now find to have overspread the earth. "Run to and fro in the streets of Jerusalem, and see if ye can find a man," a man that loveth the Lord his God with all his heart, and serveth him with all his strength.

often are never brought to justice. No-one could count all the profanities, blasphemies, lies, slander, evil speech, Sabbath-breaking, greed, drunkenness, vengefulness, prostitutions, adulteries, sexual sins, frauds, injustices, oppressions and extortions which have covered this country like a flood.[60]

3:11. Even among those who have kept themselves pure from the greater sins, there is still so much anger and pride, so much apathy and laziness, so much cross-gender behaviour and homosexuality, so much obscene luxury and self-indulgence, so much envy and selfish ambition, so much thirst for praise, so much love of the world, and so much fear of people to be found! Meanwhile, how little of true Christianity there is! Can anyone show me someone who loves God or

---

[60] How does our own land mourn (that we look no farther) under the overflowings of ungodliness! What villainies of every kind are committed day by day; yea, too often with impunity, by those who sin with a high hand, and glory in their shame! Who can reckon up the oaths, curses, profaneness blasphemies; the lying, slandering, evil-speaking; the Sabbath-breaking, gluttony, drunkenness, revenge; the whoredoms, adulteries, and various uncleanness; the frauds, injustice, oppression, extortion, which overspread our land as a flood

their neighbour as the Bible commands? On one side are those who don't even act Christian, and on the other there are those who act Christian but inside are completely dead like a painted coffin.[61]

Anyone who honestly observed any English Christian meeting (Anglican ones included) would easily see that half the congregation are Sadducees and the other half Pharisees. One side cares so little about their faith that they don't even believe in resurrection, angels and spirits, and other reduces their faith to a lifeless shell; a dead routine of faithless superficial acts without love for God or joy in the Holy Spirit.[62]

---

[61]   11. And even among those who have kept themselves pure from those grosser abominations; how much anger and pride how much sloth and idleness, how much softness and effeminacy how much luxury and self-indulgence, how much covetousness and ambition, how much thirst of praise, how much love of the world, how much fear of man, is to be found! Meanwhile, how little of true religion! For, where is he that loveth either God or his neighbour, as he hath given us commandment On the one hand, are those who have not so much as the form of godliness; on the other, those who have the form only: there stands the open, there the painted, sepulchre.

[62]   So that in very deed, whosoever were earnestly to behold any public gathering together of the people (I fear those in our churches are not to be excepted) might easily perceive, "that the one part were Sadducees,

3:12. I wish to God that we weren't this way too! Brothers and sisters, my desire and prayer is that you will be saved from this tidal wave of sin and that its flood waters will not reach you. But have they reached you? God knows, and our consciences agree that they have.[63]

You haven't kept yourselves pure. We too are corrupt and depraved, and there are very few Christians left who truly understand and worship God in spirit and in truth. We too are a generation who don't set our hearts as we should, and whose spirits don't cling firmly to God. He has told us to be *'the salt of the earth. But what good is salt if it has lost its flavour?*

---

and the other Pharisees": the one having almost as little concern about religion, as if there were "no resurrection, neither angel nor spirit;" and the other making it a mere lifeless form, a dull round of external performances, without either true faith, or the love of God, or joy in the Holy Ghost!

[63]   12. Would to God I could except us of this place! "Brethren, my heart's desire, and prayer to God, for you is, that ye may be saved" from this overflowing of ungodliness; and that here may its proud waves be stayed! But is it so indeed God knoweth, yea, and our own consciences, it is not.

Can you make it salty again? It will be thrown out and trampled underfoot as worthless.' (Mt 5:13)[64]

3:13. *'"Should I not punish them for this?" declares the LORD. "Should I not avenge myself on such a nation as this?"'* (Jer 5:9) We do not know how soon He might send war to our land because He has given us so much time to change our ways, and we have not. He has not punished us this year so far, but He is warning us and waking us up with the distant rumble of an approaching storm. His judgements are being executed on the nations and we have every reason to expect the heaviest punishment of all.[65]

---

[64]   Ye have not kept yourselves pure. Corrupt are we also and abominable; and few are there that understand any more; few that worship God in spirit and in truth. We, too, are "a generation that set not our hearts aright, and whose spirit cleaveth not steadfastly unto God." he hath appointed us indeed to be "the salt of the earth: but if the salt hath lost its savour, it is thenceforth good for nothing; but to be cast out, and to be trodden underfoot of men."

[65]   13. And "shall I not visit for these things, saith the Lord Shall not My soul be avenged on such a nation as this" Yea, we know not how soon he may say to the sword, "Sword, go through this land!" he hath given us long space to repent. he lets us alone this year also: but he warns and awakens us by thunder. his judgements are abroad in the earth; and we have all reason to expect the heaviest of all

He might come quickly to us and remove our lamp stand from its place, unless we repent and do the things we did at first (Rev 2:5), returning to the principles of the Reformation and the truth of the gospel. It could be that we are now resisting God's last gracious effort to save us. It could be that we have just about filled up our sins to the limit by rejecting what God says about us, and by turning against His messengers.[66]

3:14. Oh God, even though you are angry, remember your mercy! Be glorified through rebuilding and reforming us, not by destroying us! Let us *'Heed the rod and the One who appointed it!'* (Mic 6:9) Now that your punishments are falling on the world, let the people learn how to live righteously![67]

---

[66]   even that he "should come unto us quickly, and remove our candlestick out of its place, except we repent and do the first works;" unless we return to the principles of the Reformation, the truth and simplicity of the gospel. Perhaps we are now resisting the last effort of divine grace to save us. Perhaps we have well-nigh "filled up the measure of our iniquities," by rejecting the counsel of God against ourselves, and casting out his messengers.

[67]   14. O God, "in the midst of wrath, remember mercy!" Be glorified in our reformation, not in our destruction! Let us "hear the rod,

3:15. My family, it is high time we woke up from our sleep before the great trumpet of the Lord is blown, and our land is reduced to fields filled with dead bodies. Oh, may we quickly see what will bring us peace, before it is taken away! Turn us around, Oh good Lord, and let your anger towards us end.[68]

Oh Lord, look down from heaven. Come to England and cause us to recognise that you are here. Help us, O God who saves, for the sake of your own reputation! Oh save us and show us mercy for our sins, for the sake of your own name![69] Change us so that we will not turn away from you. Oh, let us live, and we will call out to you. Turn us back to you, O Lord

---

and him that appointed it!" Now that Thy "judgements are abroad in the earth," let the inhabitants of the world "learn righteousness!"

[68]   15. My brethren, it is high time for us to awake out of sleep before the "great trumpet of the Lord be blown," and our land become a field of blood. O may we speedily see the things that make for our peace, before they are hid from our eyes! "Turn Thou us, O good Lord, and let Thine anger cease from us.

[69]   O Lord, look down from heaven, behold and visit this vine;" and cause us to know "the time of our visitation." "Help us, O God of our salvation, for the glory of Thy name!

God of Heaven's Armies! Let your face shine upon us, and we will be complete.

Now all glory to God, who is able, through his mighty power at work within us, to accomplish infinitely more than we might ask or think. Glory to him in the church and in Christ Jesus through all generations forever and ever! Amen![70]

---

[70]   O deliver us, and be merciful to our sins, for Thy name's sake! And so we will not go back from Thee. O let us live, and we shall call upon Thy name. Turn us again, O Lord God of Hosts! Show the light of Thy countenance, and we shall be whole."

"Now unto him that is able to do exceeding abundantly above all that we can ask or think, according to the power that worketh in us, unto him be glory in the church by Christ Jesus throughout all ages; world without end. --Amen!"

Printed in Great Britain
by Amazon